T0128369

Fifty Important Things
You Should Know about
LIFE AND BUSINESS

*Or Things Your Boss or Parents
Should Have Told You*

PM Ryan

ISBN: 978-1-4669-2889-3 (sc)
ISBN: 978-1-4669-2890-9 (e)

Trafford rev. 04/10/2012

 www.trafford.com

North America & international
toll-free: 1 888 232 4444 (USA & Canada)
phone: 250 383 6864 ♦ fax: 812 355 4082

FORWARD

This compilation of thoughts has been in the works for over 40 years. The ideas are certainly not all original, and some of them you have probably seen in different venues and learning sessions. They are, however, the most relevant and specific ones in my experience—being effective for both personal and business success. Another disclaimer is that I was not always successful in following my own advice in all cases, but aside from that human frailty, the principles are still valid. I hope you find them interesting, slightly humorous, and potentially valuable to your own life and work situations. I have also interspersed some photos I have taken over the course of time, hope you enjoy them also.

The one thing you can't ever lose is integrity. It is the single most important trait you have and the one that turns all the others meaningless if you don't have it or if you lose it along the way.

You can't get to the future without letting go of your past. Your past is only important to get you where you are now—your co-workers and bosses really don't want to hear what you did, only what you are going to do now and in the future. The more you live in the past, the more likely your current job will also be part of the past.

Concentrate on your desired outcome. Most people get lost along the path of a complicated process or difficult journey and lose sight of what they were really trying to accomplish. In a meeting for instance, don't make winning an argument with someone your desired outcome—work on achieving what you went there to accomplish. Instead of trying to annihilate your peer, try to move them in a direction that achieves an outcome. Don't let side roads make you miss the goal.

W ork highest priorities. Pay some attention to the next. Ignore the lowest. If you are good at what you do, time is the most valuable resource you have. The most productive person in the room is usually the one with the most to do. If I had to pick the best person to get a critical task done, I tried to pick the busiest (and most successful, not just busy). But in doing so, help prioritize so that the lowest priorities can be ignored or displaced to help create time for the highest priorities.

Always take the high road. Going negative almost always come back around to you. No matter how irritated you are, don't send that email, don't yell, don't demean, don't lose your temper, etc. You can be firm without losing integrity and respect.

One of the most critical elements of a business relationship is to set agreed expectations. Many individuals performing a contract or overseeing a contract rely on intuition and perception more than an agreed expectation of outcome. It is hard to have the conversation about what you can and cannot accomplish, because most people want to "please" their customers. You will please them more by being direct about what you will provide, what you will not, and then meet or exceed those agreed expectation.

Feelings are not facts. Just listen to the daily political shows and you will know what I am trying to say here. Separate what you want to be true from what you know you can defend in business. Wishing is not a strategic plan.

In business, every person is temporary. In life, every person should be considered permanent. Business loyalty exists but is based on value added to each other. When the value ceases, so does the relationship, thus making the relationship temporary. In personal relationships however, there may well be a long-term relationship based on family, past history, or other compelling items that carry well beyond immediate business value. Recognize the difference between personal and business relationships. And when you leave a position, you are gone—don't ever think you were indispensible. Someone can always replace you. Perhaps not the same exact way, but in their own way. One of the true tests of friendships is if your "friend" reaches out to you after you are gone and they don't have a compelling need. Those that reach out, consider as friends. Those that don't, consider them past acquaintances.

You can't overcome stupid. Lots of different ways of saying this but it is true. The trick is to recognize whether the source of the issue can be changed or not. If so, help overcome. If not, recognize it and move on. But don't spend a lot of time on it or you violate the principle of time being the most important asset you have.

Many people are just not happy unless they are unhappy or mad. There are people like this— understand it and recognize it, because you can't change them. Nor should you try. Just deal with it.

Staffs give briefings, executives make decisions. Short and simple advice that every person in a leadership role needs to relearn every meeting and conversation. Staffs, including lawyers, are there to give advice. They are not ultimately responsible for the decision so their advice is unconstrained.

Executives, however, are responsible for the outcome and must take responsibility for the decisions within their area of responsibility.

Engineering excellence does not always translate into business. As a friend (TMorgan) of mine often said—a good engineer will always build "something"—it is up to you do help make that "something" useful. There are many good ideas; there are fewer good business outcomes.

Perspective. Don't treat every action as transactional. By that I mean only pertaining to that specific event or action. Treat your actions within the context of your goals, your priorities, your desired outcomes and your desired legacy. Don't lose yourself in the moment.

Perspective is great—this is NY City at sunset

Ryan's rules of teenage hood (deny, blame, compare). This is a take off from Sigmund Freud so there is historical truth to it. When you look at business and problems associated with business or people, you can compare it to how my teenagers looked at issues. When confronted with something they did but shouldn't have, teenagers exhibit common responses. First they deny it—wasn't me! If you can prove it was them, they move to blaming someone else—John made me do it! And if you get by that one, the third character response is to compare it to something worse that gets them off the hook—well, last week Mary did so and so and you didn't ground her so why are you picking on me? By this time, you are out of energy and time and simply move on, leaving them alone. This works for teenagers to a tee, and many people retain these traits in adulthood—recognize when it is occurring and you will be ahead of the game.

Short is better than long. Most of us find this hard to execute, because when you are not absolutely sure what you want to say, you take longer to say it or write it. Emails, speeches, conferences, meetings, etc. But attention spans are short, people are time constrained and are becoming so multi-tasked that anything longer than a tweet is more than they can absorb. Keep it as short as you can to gain the desired outcome.

Do what you say or don't say it. Don't speak out just because you think your comment is the right thing to say. If you can't execute on it, hold that thought to yourself.

O wn it or Kill it. Recognize that many people in business have a binary outlook at initiatives. There are those that relate all business to a personal view—and believe that any initiative presented should either be theirs (under their sponsorship and control), or killed so that it doesn't compete with "their" initiative. Many are successful in business with this approach because it is decisive and gives the appearance of "good" leadership by prioritizing. While agreeing that prioritizing is good, don't let someone kill an initiative because it can't be made in his or her own image or control.

Teamwork at its best—thousands of people working
towards the same mission and outcome

Circular vs. Direct Thought. There are lots of different kinds of thinkers in life and in business. Two of them think in patterns that I relate to "circular" and "direct". The direct thinker wants to connect two dots by the most direct path, get right to the outcome, and move on. They are usually easy to work with and easy to spot because you know exactly what they are thinking. On the other hand, the "circular" thinker doesn't telegraph what they want for an outcome, they try to lead others down paths that get to their desired outcome without it being obvious. They are more dangerous, because you might not know you are heading down their path and might not agree with the prize at the end of their rainbow.

Focus on the path, not the obstacles along the way

Its hard work being an alcoholic. You might wonder what this has to do with business. My point is that it is hard work to do anything well—even being an alcoholic. You have to continuously work at it, perfecting how to do it, staying on target with desired outcome, not getting distracted, and achieving desired goals. When you start to lose that focus, think of this bit of advice on how hard it is to stay focused on being an alcoholic!

Short dress syndrome—blame the easiest person to blame. This is an observation of my dear wife who taught at the high school, and other, levels for many years. It is an interesting phenomenon that a manager/administrator would rather discipline the ones that will accept the discipline much more than those who are combative. So to explain—say the Vice Principal finds an otherwise respectful girl whose dress is too short in their view. The VP finds it easy to address the issues and discipline because the girl doesn't make it a huge issue in return. On the other hand, say the same VP finds a student who has a history of combativeness, family involvement in all the wrong ways, and knows that student will make whatever the VP does or says a major issue through the school, the board of education, and any other possible way to cause pain. In this case the VP moves on without calling out the student. So the result is the "good" girl with minor infractions gets nailed, and the worse offender is not. Business is sometimes the same situation—unless you have the time, you might not address an issue that you know will take up a great deal of future time to resolve, even if it is a more deserving issue to resolve. Don't let yourself fall into that trap.

Doing something you believe in rather than being paid to do. Self explanatory and obvious but you would be amazed at how many people do things they don't believe in to make money. It gives no job satisfaction and creates rationalization at its finest. If you believe in what you are doing, you will be much happier and so will your family.

View from the lift line—even the journey to the top is enjoyable!

The years go by quickly, the days slowly, and sometimes the minutes last forever. You won't relate to this one unless you have some age and experience under your belt. If you get the point, you are there. If you don't, reread it in a couple of years ☺

Talk to the person not the subject. The discussion may be about a subject but the outcome will be based on how you address it with a real person. Have a discussion, not a competition of words.

P riorities. Similar to perspective, but taking it one step further by organizing what matters the most to you, keeping that in mind and working on them in priority order.

This bird has priorities and is focused!

Vision—know where you are going. If you have a good perspective and ability to prioritize, you probably also have an idea of where you want to go and how you want to get there. This matches vision, strategy, and tactics all together. Vision is the idea of where you want to go and it is powerful. It is not sufficient just to have a vision, however. There are many in business who can dream, but fewer that can implement a dream.

Learn how to say no well, but also how to say yes well. I am too often astounded at people who continue to argue their case after the other party agrees. Quit when you get what you want, say thanks and move on.

S trategy—what happens now, in a while, and finally. Otherwise known as short, medium and long-term strategy. Each of them is valuable and tying them together actually gives you the path you want.

These birds are developing short-term strategy!

People often say that there are no dumb questions! Maybe so, but there are many questions that simply are not helpful to the task. You don't have to belittle the questioner, but you also shouldn't spend much time on questions that have no relevance to the desired outcome or activity. You can get sidetracked easily by treating everything with equal importance.

Business leadership is about leading the business. There are innumerable "leadership" techniques, courses, and books. Most concentrate on how to "train" a person to become a leader. You can train a manager, but a leader has to learn to lead through his or her own actions.

Be decisive on things that matter—not on trivia. Don't try to demonstrate leadership and decisiveness on minutia. People will recognize it and your effectiveness will be diminished. Hold your ground on matters of importance. Often you can let less important matters be training ground for your employees—you can let them fail and learn on those matters.

Never think someone is gone. They well could come back in a different time and venue and they WILL remember how you treated them.

Really smart people don't have to prove it. You know the type that just has to prove how much they know every time they speak—now think about how you really can't stand that! The smartest people I have ever known are the ones that made the substance carry the day vice the speech.

You can't "manage" change—you can welcome it. Business, people, markets, technology, etc.—all change at Internet speed. You can't change it or slow it down (except in your own mind☺). Embrace change as part of life and business—and make the best of the changes as they occur.

Motivation: People are motivated by:

1. Their own internal compass (back to the integrity point).
2. Their family, friends, leaders and mentors.
3. Appreciation. Say thank you more often—people appreciate being appreciated (emphasized to me by CDecarlo).
4. Their incentives—pay, promotions, etc. I have been told often that people do what they get paid for. I agree that people will often work the most on what they are rewarded for, but too many self-created leaders think that people will only work on money related outcomes. Pay makes a difference but it isn't the only incentive that matters and those that think it is are thinking short and tactical.

Profit is not a four-letter word, but loss is. You can't continue working on things that don't produce a return. The reason is that your company will either go away or you will!

Reserve the right to get smarter. Keep learning every day. Part of the reward of working in a great company or organization is that you can learn from your coworkers and leaders.

Pick a path—where do you want to go and
how do you want to get there?

B e a compass, not a weather vane. Back to the
integrity and internal compass points. A weather
vane agrees with every new gust of wind. A compass
knows where true North lies.

Just because you CAN be in charge doesn't mean you SHOULD. Most people believe they should keep moving up the management chain because that is the next level for which to strive. What they don't often analyze is whether they really want what goes with the new job promotion. I have seen many people promoted beyond either their capabilities or beyond their desire to manage/lead. It is not easy to manage people, if that is not your strong point, don't ask to be a manager.

I have learned so much over the years; I just wish I could remember it. You are probably too young to recognize the truth to this adage, but as you get older, you will agree. Don't think that because you knew something once, you still do ☺

Transmitting does not mean the other side is receiving. How many times have you spoken and the other person just doesn't seem to be getting it? The cause could be you, your method of conveying the message, or it just plain could be them. Think of it as a radio. You can transmit if you are turned on, but that doesn't mean there is anyone listening. It's up to you to insure that you have the right situation set up to both transmit and receive. And remember—it's hard to discuss anything with someone who knows it all already!

Don't gain the sale of the moment and lose the business. Many people in business have sales metrics—numbers to meet. The goal is to make the sale to make the bonus. It is natural and not bad—it is how companies work and how they stay profitable. However, if the immediate sale gets you to the number in a way that puts future business at risk, it is detrimental to all.

Pain versus value matrix. In working with my teams over the years, I developed a team dynamic where I would create quadrants of where to put team members (and shared it with them). Below is the graph:

High Value - Low Pain (Best types to have)	High Value - High Pain (These types can create both high return and high conflict—you MUST manage them well)
Low Value - Low Pain (These types can slide at times but not for all time)	Low Value - High Pain (These folks will be weeded out)

Don't turn every conversation into a competition. You know the type—they not only have to be right, they have to win the argument at all costs. Learn from others; don't try to defeat everyone in every conversation.

Don't Polish a BB! Meaning that once the idea or goal is accomplished, don't keep working on it. Once that BB is the way you want it, move on, it doesn't do you any good to make it more polished.

It is easier to disagree or criticize than it is to agree or help. I can find fault with anything, but it won't move the goal forward. Constructive criticism is valuable but insure that criticism isn't the only desired approach. At some point you need to agree, move out, and succeed.

Saying no is an art. You can easily overdo or underdo the tendency to disagree. It is not a badge of honor to always disagree, nor is being a yes person the desired outcome. Learn how and when to say no/disagree in a way that moves the organization forward and you retain your integrity. If you can't do both, perhaps it is time to move on.

People are never more communicative and collaborative then when they are looking for jobs. I can't tell you how many people would not give me the time of day until they were looking for a career change and wanted help.

We should all be on the same page usually means, "You need to agree with me". It is like the current political meaning of bi-partisan. All will never be "on the same page" but it is necessary to agree on desired outcomes and methods of achieving.

In the beginning, the middle, and the end, it is all about relationships! Achievements have no meaning without the people behind the achievements. You will find lasting relationships much more rewarding than any of the temporary rewards you sought along the way.

Relationships make the journey!

CONCLUSION

I hope you have enjoyed reading this. I tried to keep it short (one of the principles) and with a bit of humor. If it helps you in business or in your personal life, my goal is accomplished. Thank you for reading it.

Is this a sunset or a sunrise?—
Either the start or the end of a day?
Either way it is beautiful

ACKNOWLEDGEMENTS

My most heartfelt thanks to my wife, LuAnne, and our five children (Cinnamon, Bromlyn, Erin, Wes, and Maren) for their patience and love throughout my working career and many travels away from home. They helped me grow into a better person than I could have ever done by myself.

A double rainbow at the beach with my partner in life!

Printed in the United States
By Bookmasters